Table of Contents

D1456076

Super Sentences

Use the rabbit box and the carrot shape to encourage children to create sentences that are more than "The rabbit ran."

Preparing the Center:

1. Cover the shoe box and lid in Contact paper or butcher paper.

2. Use the rabbit pattern pieces on pages 3 and 5. Laminate the pieces or cover them with clear Contact paper. Cut out all of the pieces. Use an Exacto blade to cut the slit in the head. Fold the pieces and use double-sided tape to attach them to the shoe box.

3. Reproduce the carrots (pages 7-11) on card stock or copy paper. Color the carrots and leaves with crayons or marking pens. Laminate the pieces. Cut out the carrots and place them in the rabbit box.

4. Place the box in an easily accessible place. Provide a supply of pencils, crayons, writing paper, and drawing paper. You may want to add special pencils (orange like carrots, ones with bunny heads) for children to use at the writing center.

Write Super Sentences:

Have one or two children work at this center at a time.

1. Child takes the carrots out of the box and sorts them putting all descriptive words (adjectives) in one pile, all naming words (nouns) in one pile, and all action words (verbs) in a third pile. (You may want to use the blank carrots to create adverbs if you have older or more able students.)

2. Select one or more carrots from the descriptive word pile and one word each from the naming and action word piles to use in writing a sentence about rabbits.

  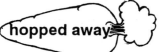 

3. Have the child see how many different sentences he/she can create using the carrots; then select one sentence to illustrate.

Rabbit Pattern - Head

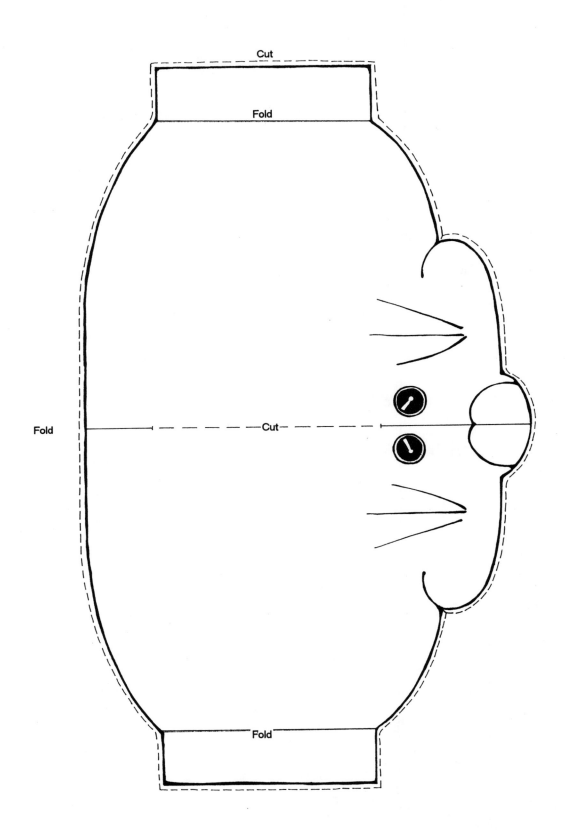

Pattern - Tail, Feet and Ears

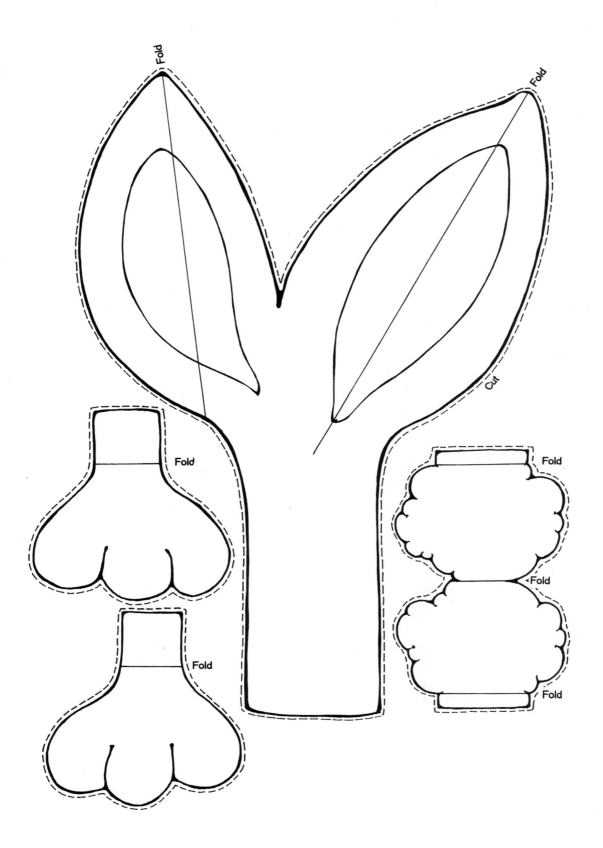

Fold

Fold

Cut

Fold

Fold

Fold

Fold

Fold

Fold

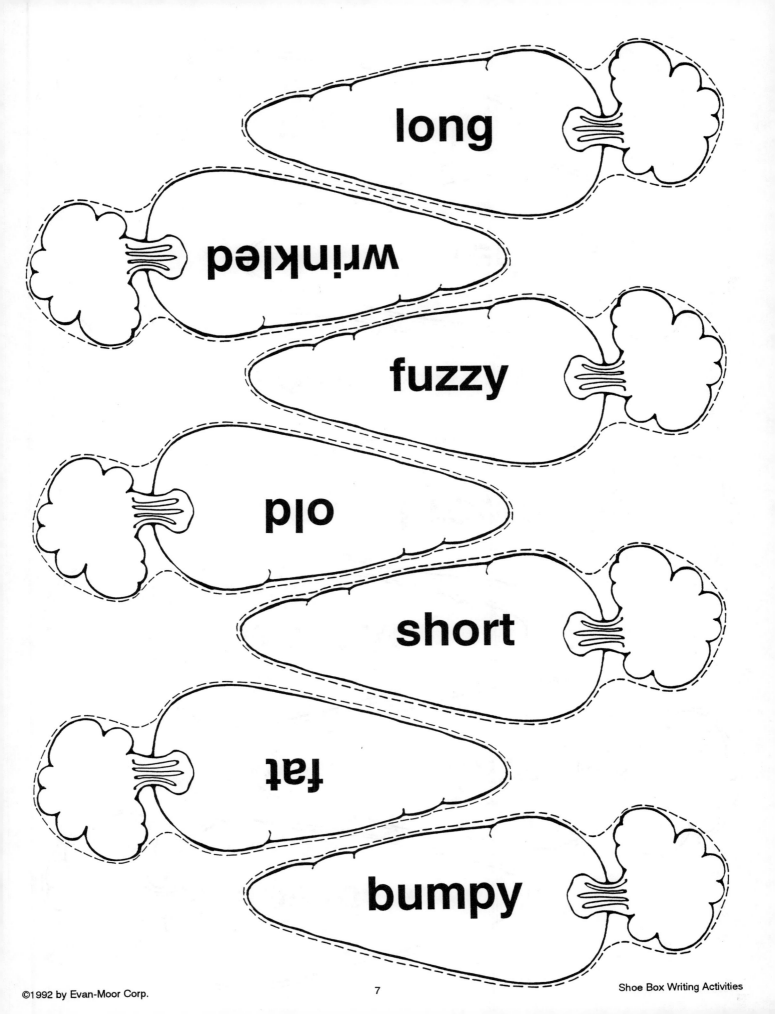

long

wrinkled

fuzzy

old

short

fat

bumpy

Shoe Box Writing Activities

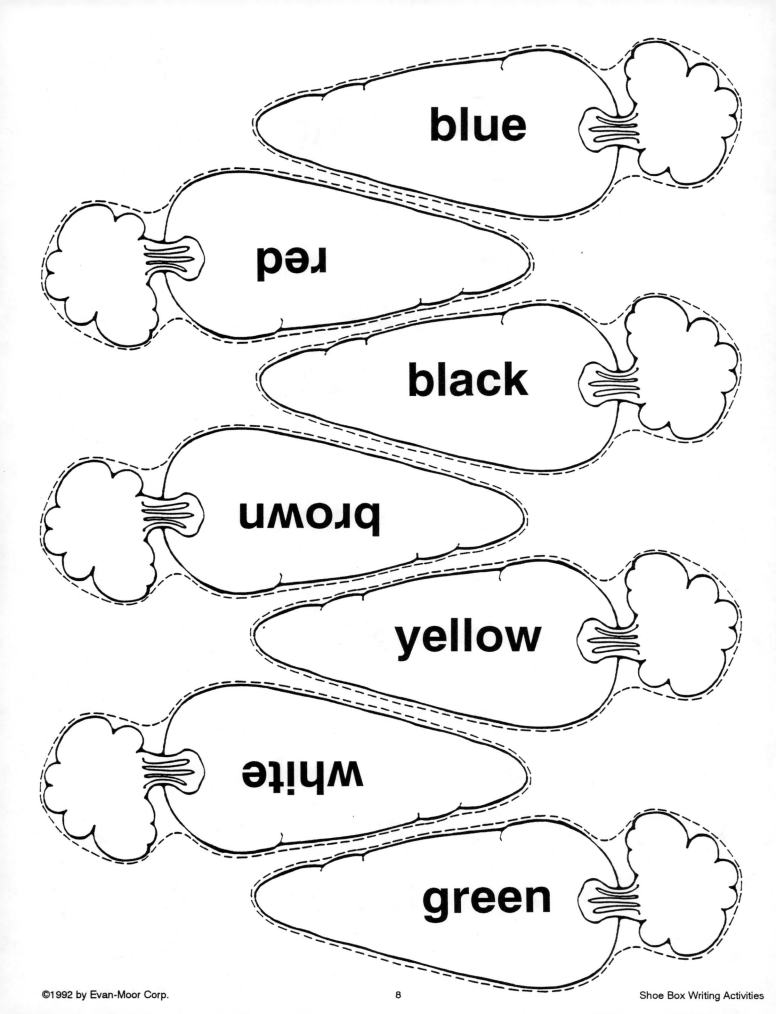

blue

red

black

brown

yellow

white

green

8

Shoe Box Writing Activities

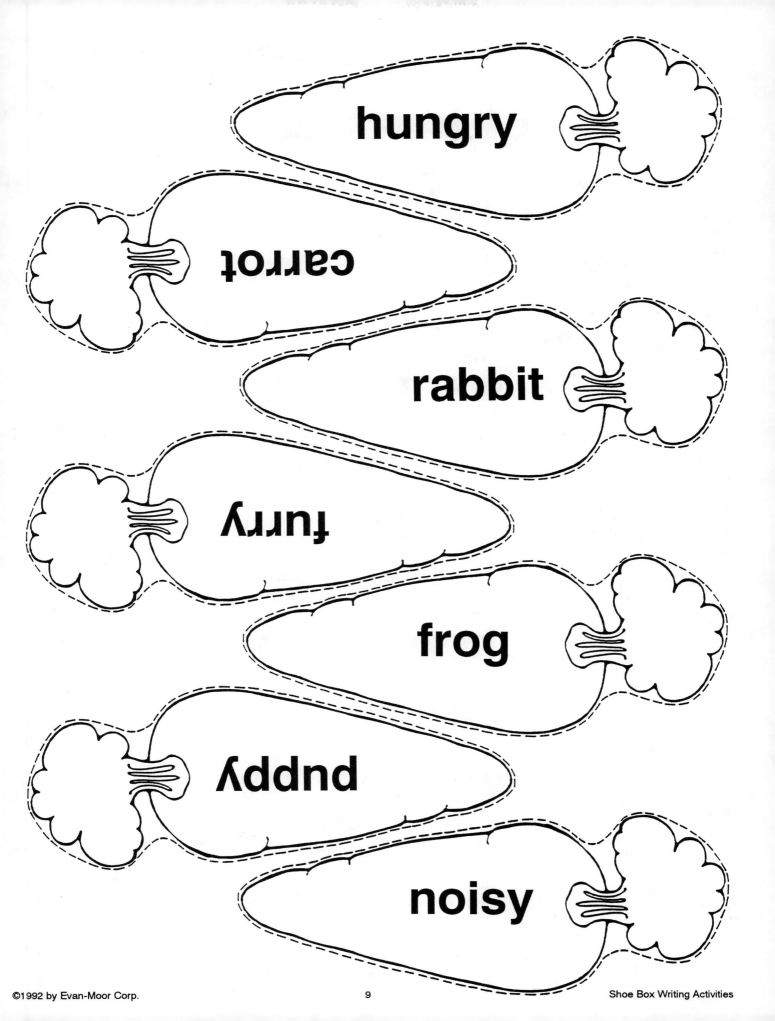

hungry

carrot

rabbit

furry

frog

puppy

noisy

Shoe Box Writing Activities

bumblebee

tastes good

went to sleep

flew

hopped away

sat down

can run

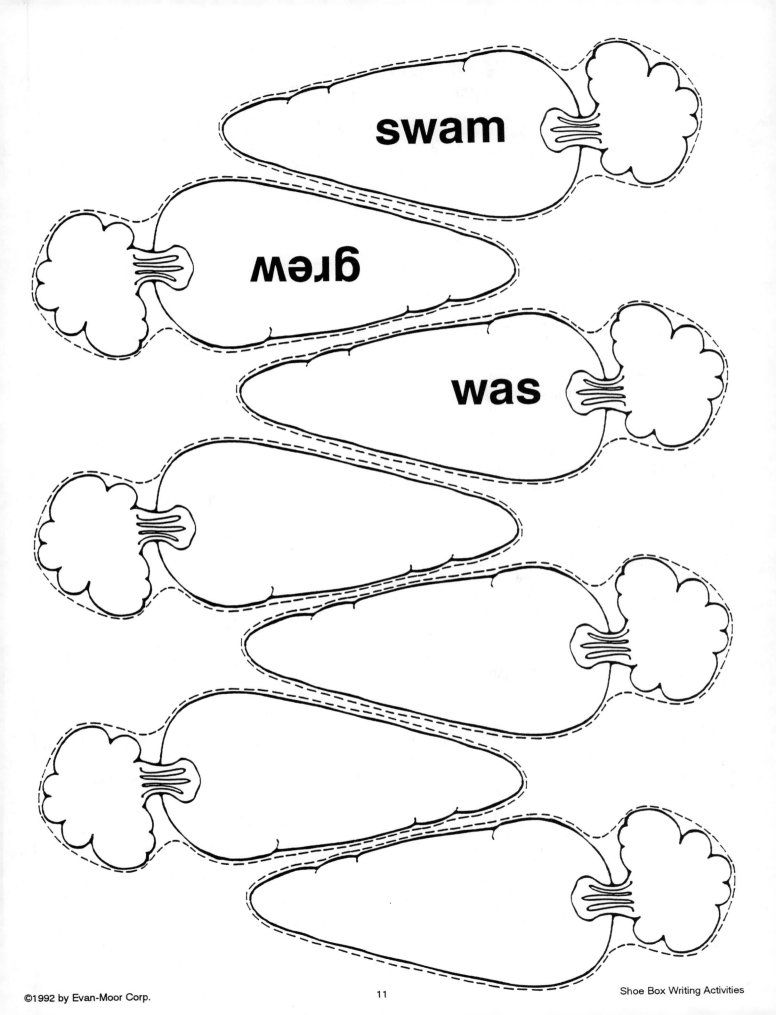

swam

grew

was

11

Descriptive Paragraphs

Use the bird house box and bird shapes to encourage children to create paragraphs describing birds and bird activities.

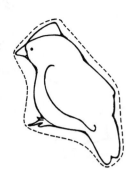

Preparing the Center:

1. Cover the shoe box and lid in Contact paper or butcher paper.

2. Use the bird house pattern on page 13. Laminate the bird house or cover it with clear Contact paper. Cut it out and attach it to the box with double-sided tape. Use an Exacto blade to cut out the hole in the bird house.

3. Reproduce the birds (pages 15-17) on white card stock or white copy paper. Color the birds with crayon or light colored marking pens. Laminate the pieces. Cut out the birds and place them in the bird house shoe box.

4. Place the box in an easily accessible place. Provide a supply of pencils, crayons, writing paper, and drawing paper. You may want to add special pencils (in the same colors as the birds, ones with bird heads) for children to use at the writing center.

Write Descriptive Paragraphs:

Have one or two children work at this center at a time.

1. Have the child reach into the bird house and pull out a bird and read the directions written on it.

2. The directions written on the bird will explain what type of description he/she needs to write.

Tell what your favorite bird looks like.

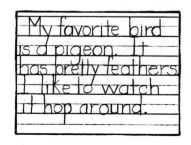

> My favorite bird is a pigeon. It has pretty feathers. I like to watch it hop around.

3. Have the child illustrate the completed paragraph.

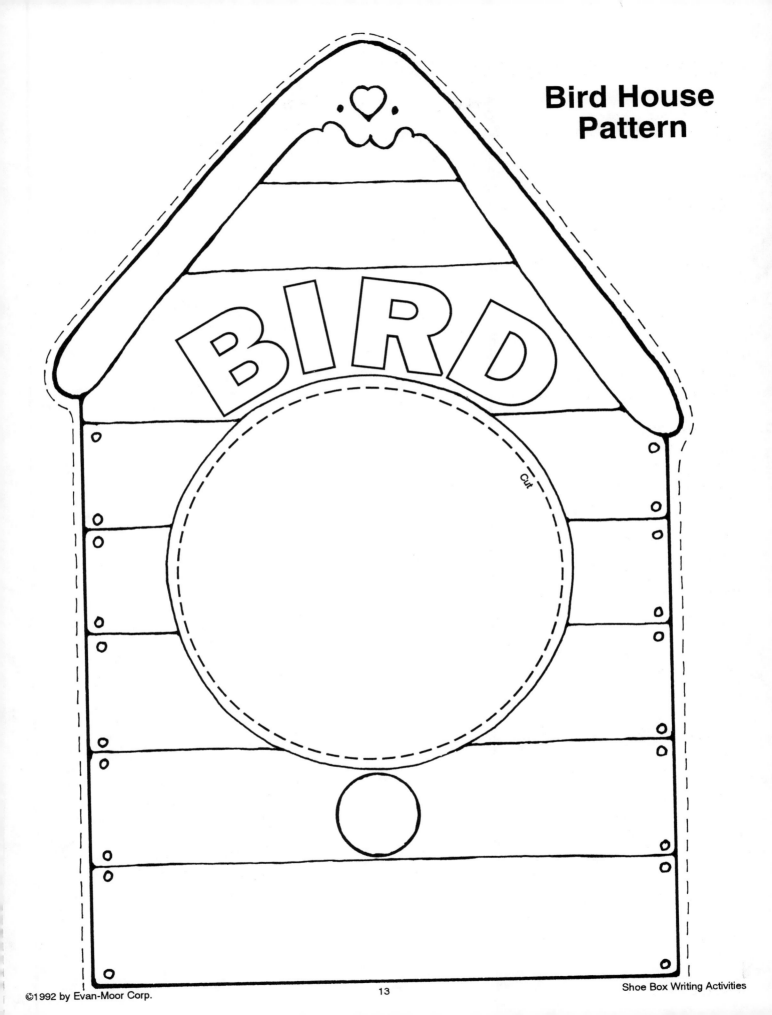

Bird House
Pattern

BIRD

Cut

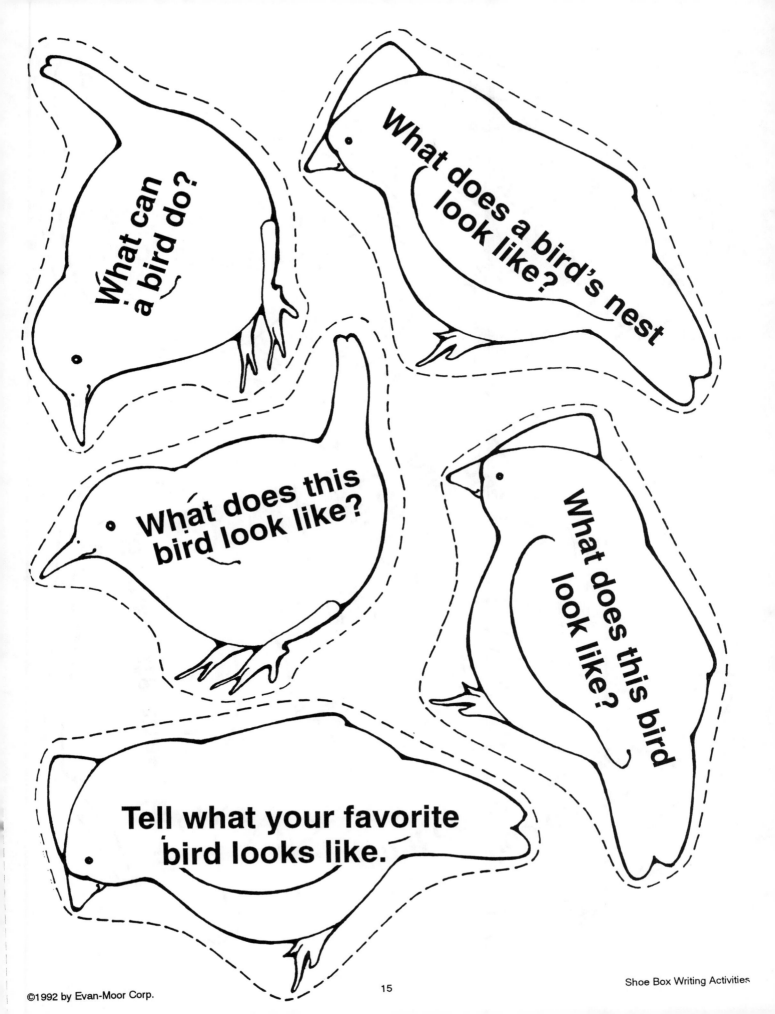

What can a bird do?

What does a bird's nest look like?

What does this bird look like?

What does this bird look like?

Tell what your favorite bird looks like.

Shoe Box Writing Activities

How does it feel
Pretend you are
a bird.

How does it feel
to fly?

Tell how a hungry
bird gets food.

Pretend you are
a bird.
What do you
look like?

Some cats chase birds.
Describe a cat.

Pretend you are a bird.
What do you like to do?

Shoe Box Writing Activities

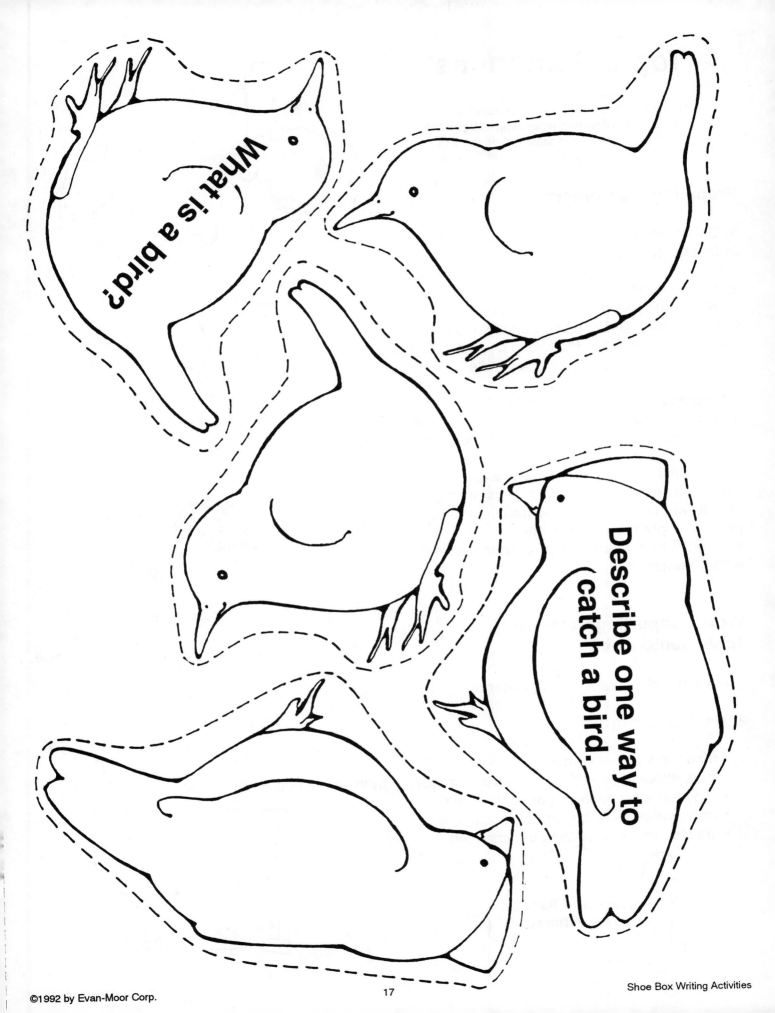

What is a bird?

Describe one way to catch a bird.

Shoe Box Writing Activities

Topic Sentences

Use the bear box and the fish shapes to encourage children to write supporting details to the topic sentences provided on the fish.

Preparing the Center:

1. Cover the shoe box and lid in Contact paper or butcher paper.

2. Use the bear pattern on page 19. Laminate the bear or cover it with clear Contact paper. Cut it out and attach it to the box with double-sided tape. Use an Exacto blade to cut out the hole in the bear's middle.

3. Reproduce the fish (pages 21-23) on colored card stock or copy paper. Laminate the pieces. Cut out the fish and place them in the bear shoe box.

4. Place the box in an easily accessible place. Provide a supply of pencils, crayons, writing paper, and drawing paper. You may want to add special pencils (bright colors, ones with fish patterns, ones with bears on the end) for children to use at the writing center.

Write Supporting Details for Topic Sentences:

Have one or two children work at this center at a time.

1. Have the child reach into the bear and pull out a fish.

2. The child should then...

- read the topic sentence
- think about supporting information that goes with the sentence
- copy the topic sentence on a piece of paper
- write one or more supporting sentences
- draw a picture illustrating the completed paragraph

Bears and fish are very different.

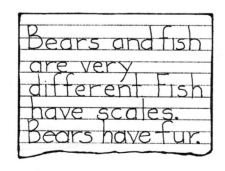

Bears and fish are very different. Fish have scales. Bears have fur.

Shoe Box Writing Activities

Bear Pattern

Cut

Shoe Box Writing Activities

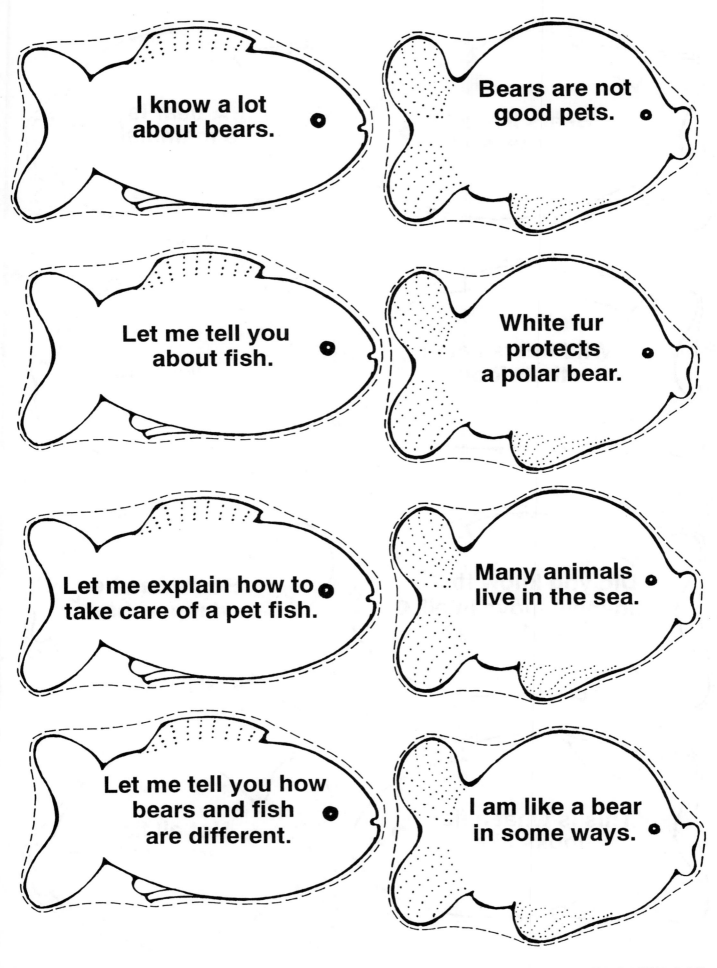

I know a lot about bears.

Bears are not good pets.

Let me tell you about fish.

White fur protects a polar bear.

Let me explain how to take care of a pet fish.

Many animals live in the sea.

Let me tell you how bears and fish are different.

I am like a bear in some ways.

Shoe Box Writing Activities

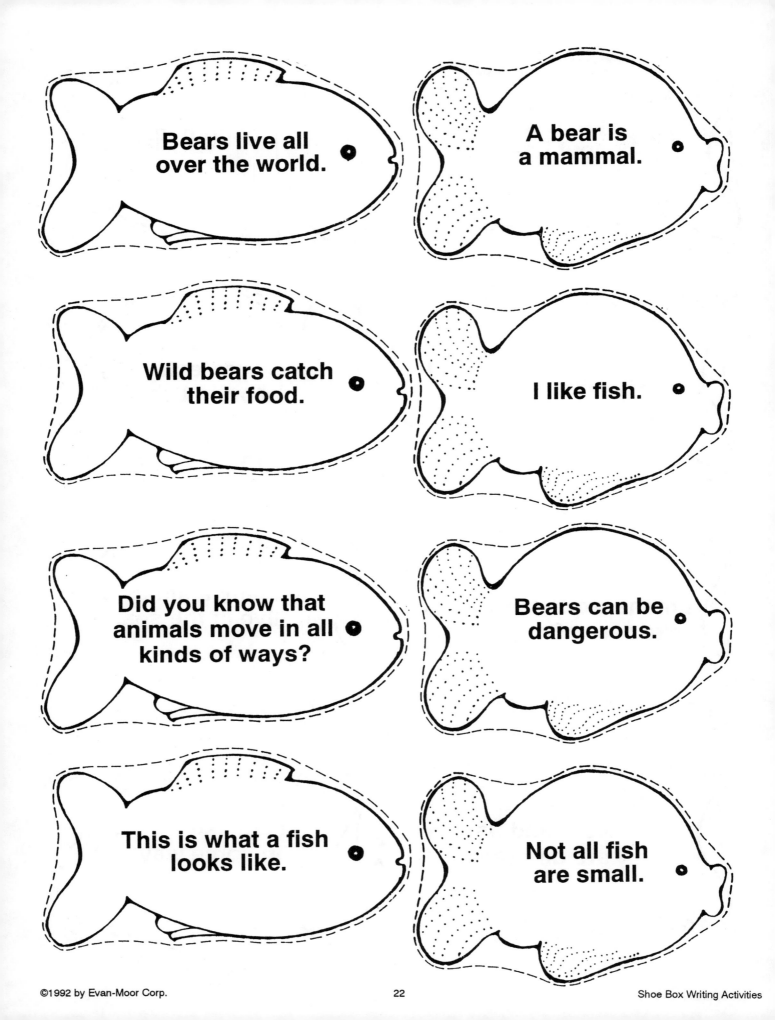

Bears live all over the world.

A bear is a mammal.

Wild bears catch their food.

I like fish.

Did you know that animals move in all kinds of ways?

Bears can be dangerous.

This is what a fish looks like.

Not all fish are small.

Shoe Box Writing Activities

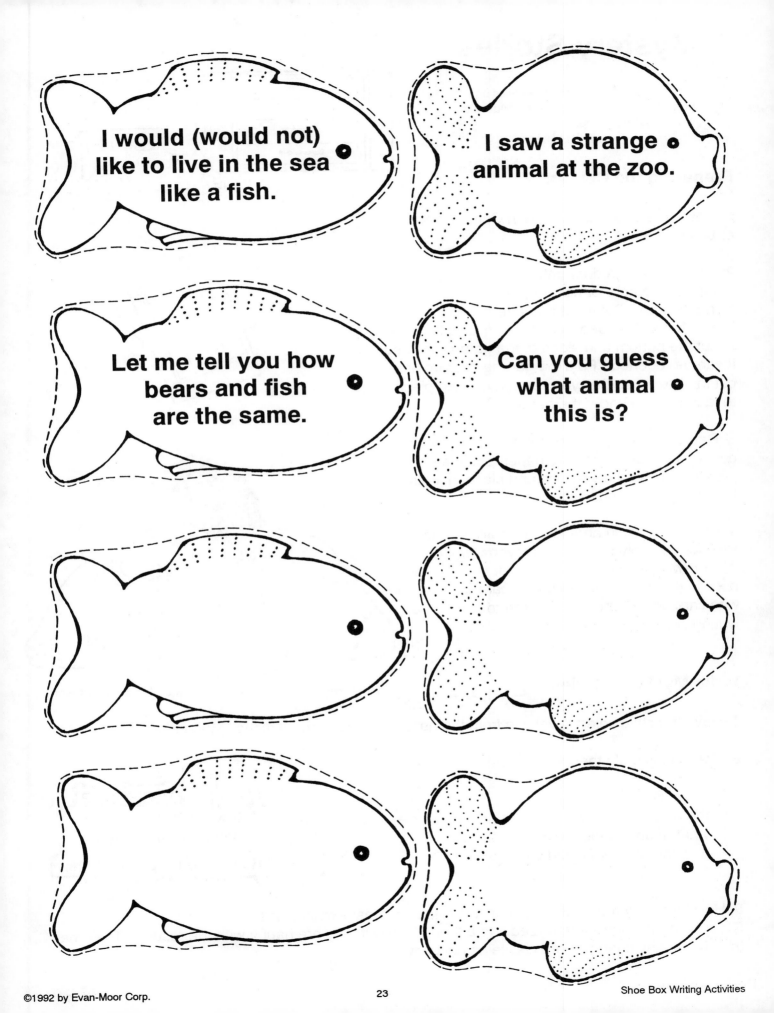

I would (would not) like to live in the sea like a fish.

I saw a strange animal at the zoo.

Let me tell you how bears and fish are the same.

Can you guess what animal this is?

Shoe Box Writing Activities

Mystery Stories

Use the garage box and the ideas on the vehicle shapes to encourage children to write mystery stories.

Preparing the Center:

1. Cover the shoe box and lid in Contact paper or butcher paper.

2. Use the garage door pattern on page 25. Laminate the door or cover it with clear Contact paper. Cut it out and attach it to the box with double-sided tape. Use an Exacto blade to cut the bottom and sides of the garage door so it can be "opened." Fold the garage door up and cut the box lid so that you can remove the piece to leave a hole under the garage door.

3. Reproduce the vehicles (pages 27-31) on colored card stock or copy paper. Laminate the pieces. Cut out the vehicles and place them in the garage shoe box.

4. Place the box in an easily accessible place. Provide a supply of pencils, crayons, writing paper, and drawing paper. You may want to add special pencils (bright colors, ones with car patterns, ones with cars on the end) for children to use at the writing center.

Write Mystery Stories:

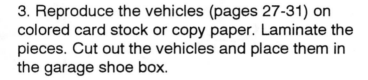

Have one or two children work at this center at a time.

1. Have the child select a vehicle from the garage and read the directions it contains.

2. The child should then think about...

- the character and/or problem on the vehicle
- what might happen to the character
- how the problem could be resolved

A boy finds a small box on the step. He picked it up. . . .

3. He/She then writes the story and illustrates the most exciting part. Older students may want to read it to a friend to see if they are happy with the results. They may then make any changes and create a final copy.

Garage Door Pattern

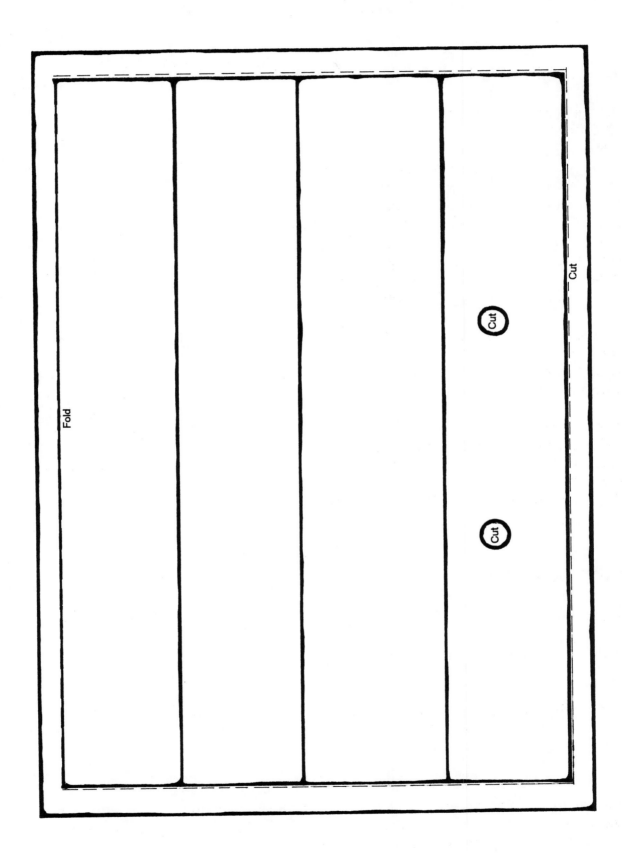

Shoe Box Writing Activities

A boy finds a small box
on the front step.

You hear a noise in the middle
of the night.

Mom is bringing a strange pet home.

Shoe Box Writing Activities

A girl looked in the mirror and saw that her face was blue.

You find a note in your library book. The note is written in code.

A light came on in the empty house next door.

 Shoe Box Writing Activities

Lunch boxes keep disappearing
at school.

Your sister and brother are doing
weird things.

They won't tell you why.

My dog dug up a strange bone.

Shoe Box Writing Activities

You find an old coat on the street.
When you look in the
pocket you find...

You see a note on your desk top
when you get to school.
It says,
"Watch this spot."

A strange ship landed on the
playground.

Shoe Box Writing Activities

31

Shoe Box Writing Activities

Nonfiction Writing

Use the tool box and the ideas on the tool shapes to encourage children to practice nonfiction writing.

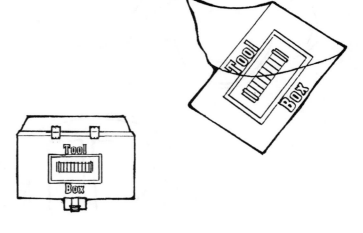

Preparing the Center:

1. Cover the shoe box and lid in Contact paper or butcher paper.

2. Use the tool box lid pattern on page 33. Laminate the lid or cover it with clear Contact paper. Cut it out and attach it to the shoe box lid with double-sided tape. Tape the back hinges of the tool box lid to the back side of the box as shown. Leave the front hinge loose. Children can then lift the box lid to get to the tools inside.

3. Reproduce the tools (pages 35-37) on colored card stock or copy paper. Laminate the pieces. Cut out the tools and place them in the tool shoe box.

4. Place the box in an easily accessible place. Provide a supply of pencils, crayons, writing paper, and drawing paper. You may want to add special pencils (bright colors, ones with car or tool patterns, ones with cars on the end) for children to use at the writing center.

Write Nonfiction Material:

Have one or two children work at this center at a time.

1. The child takes out a tool and reads the directions it contains.

2. He/She thinks about what to write, remembering that it must be true, then writes the information, set of directions, etc. called for on the tool shape.

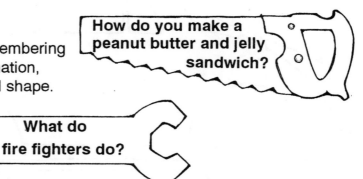

How do you make a peanut butter and jelly sandwich?

What do fire fighters do?

3. He/She may want to make an illustration to go with what has been written.

Tool Box Pattern

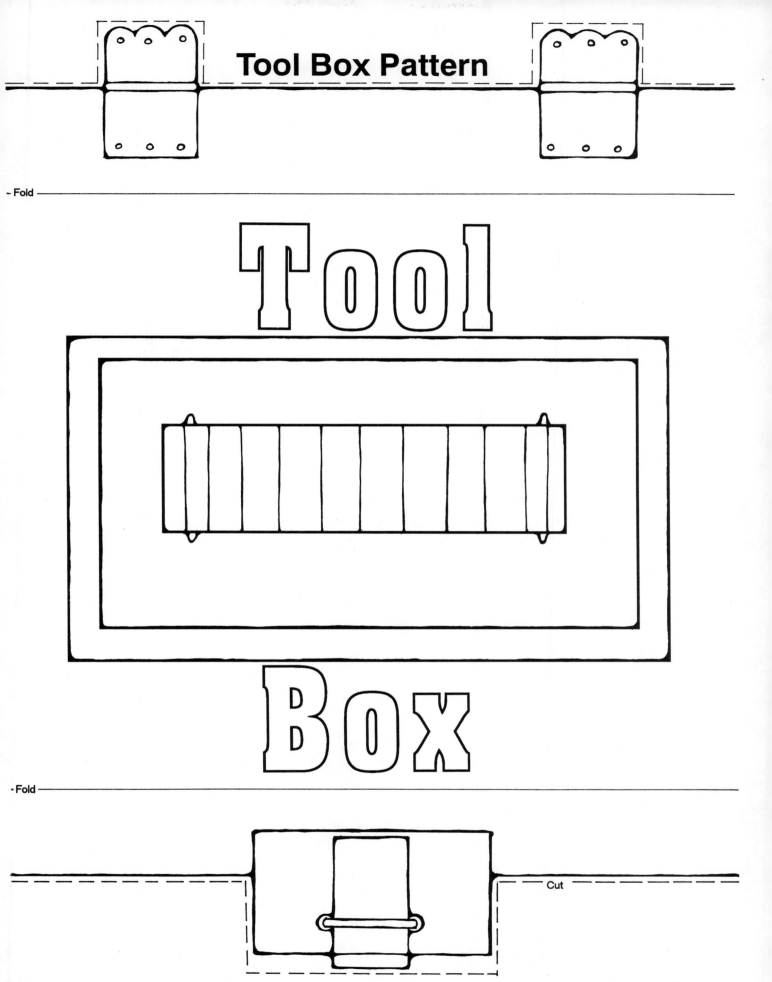

Tool
Box

Fold

Fold

Cut

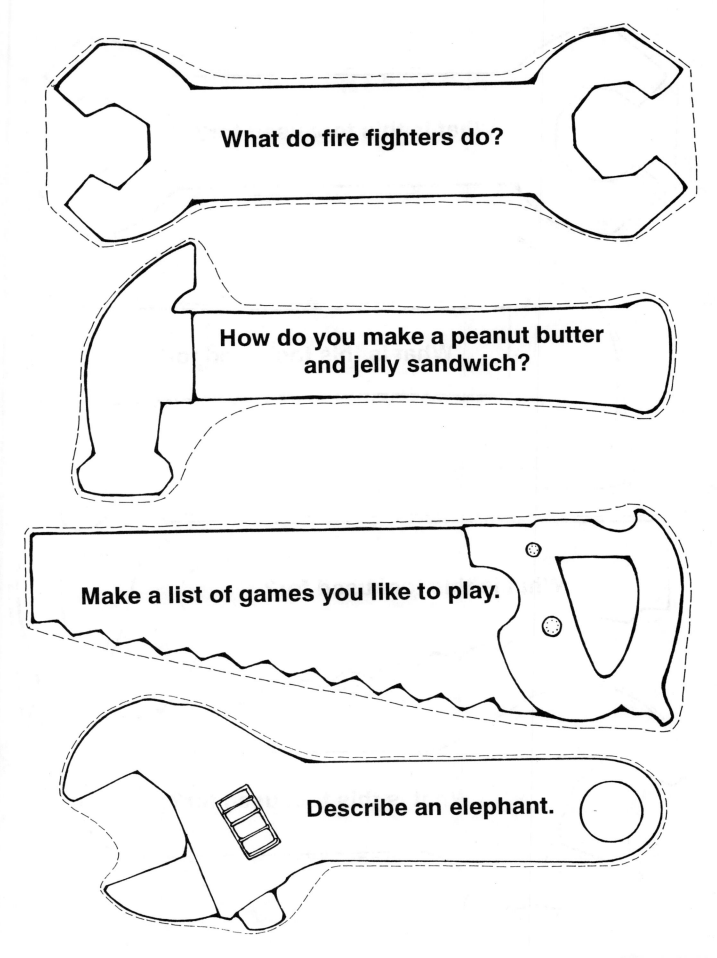

What do fire fighters do?

How do you make a peanut butter and jelly sandwich?

Make a list of games you like to play.

Describe an elephant.

Shoe Box Writing Activities

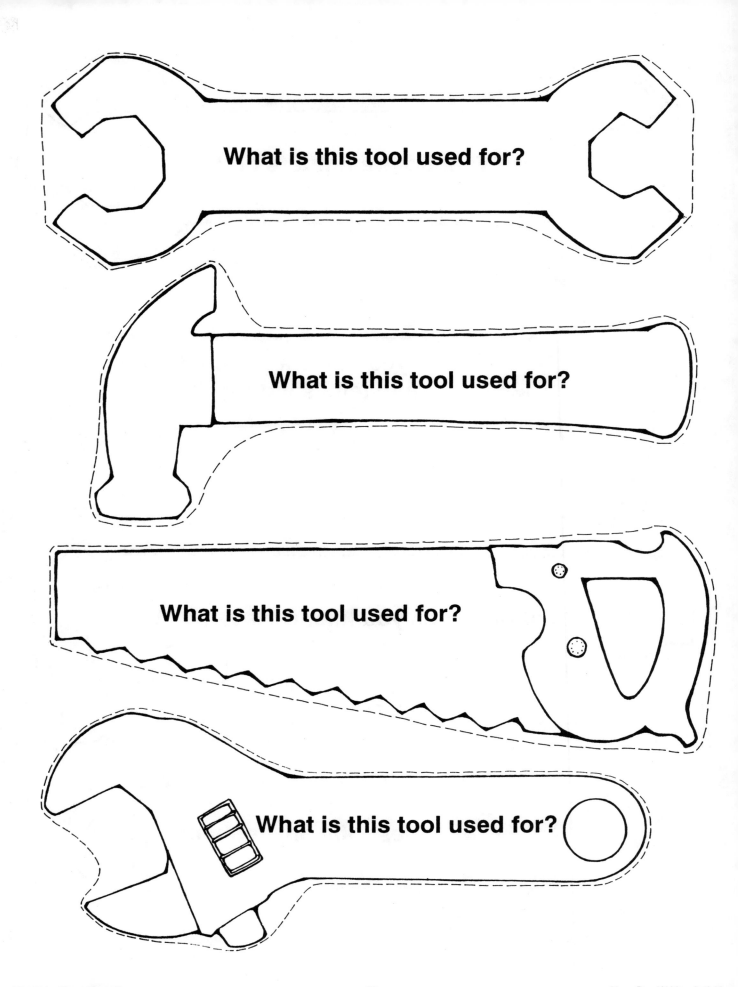

What is this tool used for?

What is this tool used for?

What is this tool used for?

What is this tool used for?

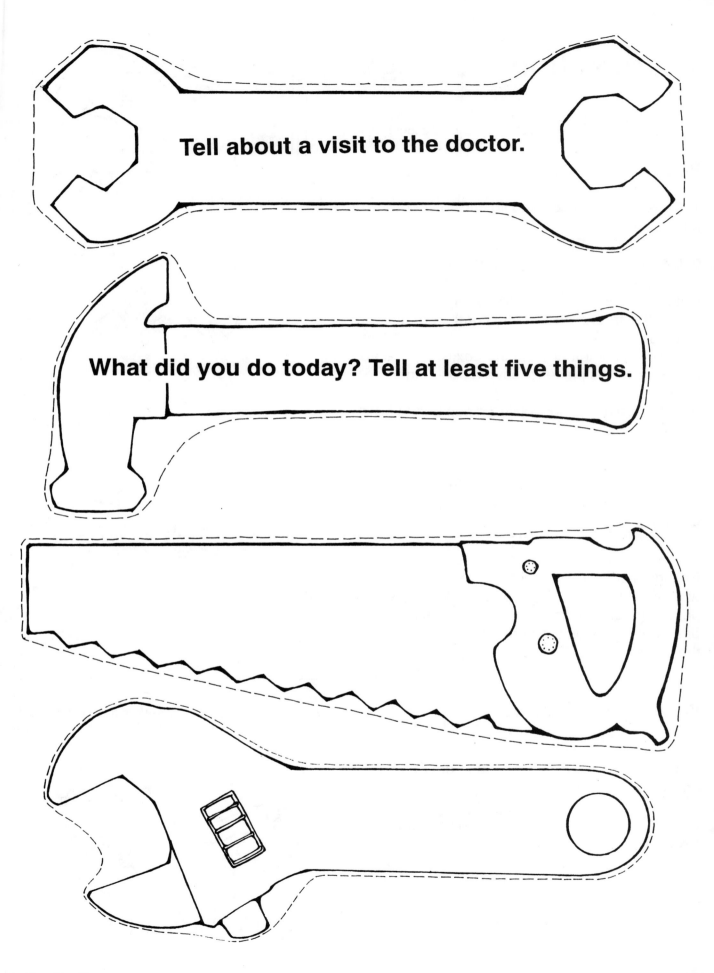

Tell about a visit to the doctor.

What did you do today? Tell at least five things.

Write about Feelings

Use the house box and the ideas on the people shapes to encourage children to write about feelings.

Preparing the Center:

1. Cover the shoe box and lid in Contact paper or butcher paper.

2. Use the house pattern on page 39. Laminate the house or cover it with clear Contact paper. Cut it out and attach it to the box with double-sided tape. Use an Exacto blade to cut the bottom and sides of the front door so it can be "opened." Fold the door to the left and cut the box lid so that you can remove the piece to leave a hole under the door. Cut out the circle where the doorknob would be. This creates a hole children can use to open the door.

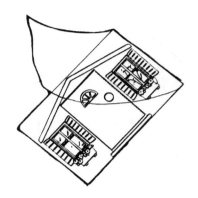

3. Reproduce the people (pages 41-43) on colored card stock or copy paper. Laminate the pieces. Cut out the people and place them in the house shoe box.

4. Place the box in an easily accessible place. Provide a supply of pencils, crayons, writing paper, and drawing paper. You may want to add special pencils (bright colors, ones with people patterns, ones with faces on the end) for children to use at the writing center.

Write about Feelings:

Have one or two children work at this center at a time.

1. The child takes a person shape out of the house and reads the directions.

2. He/She then writes about a feeling following the directions given on the shape.

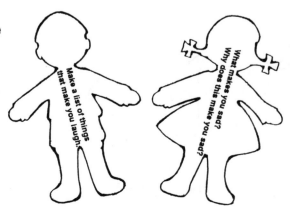

Make a list of things that make you laugh.

What makes you sad? Why does this make you sad?

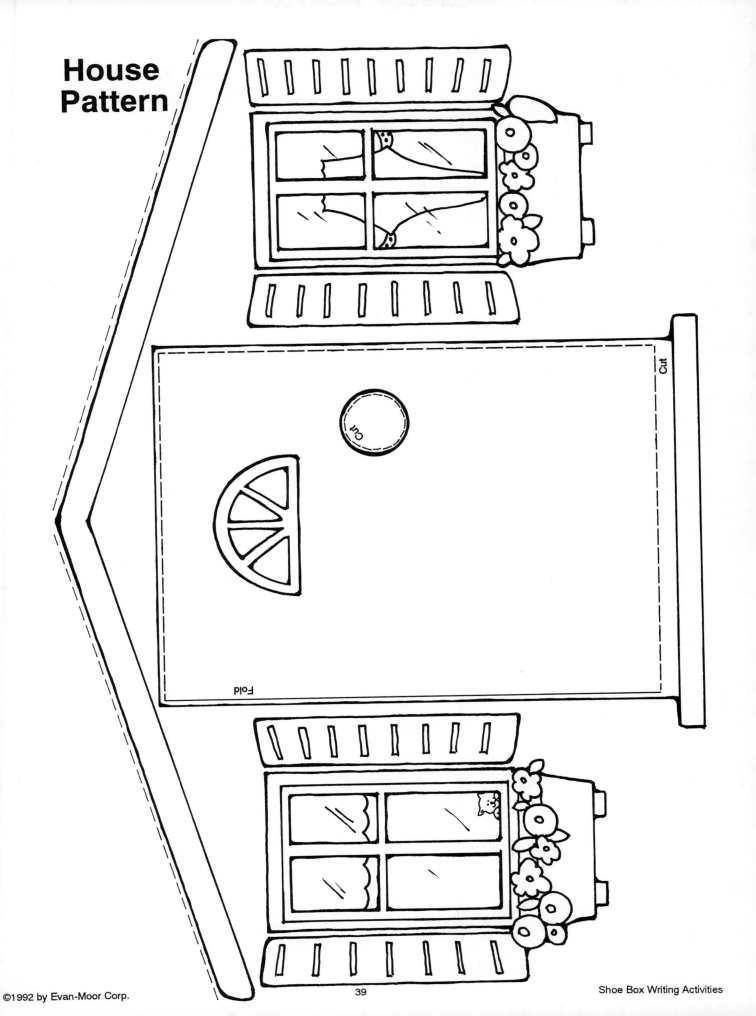

House
Pattern

39

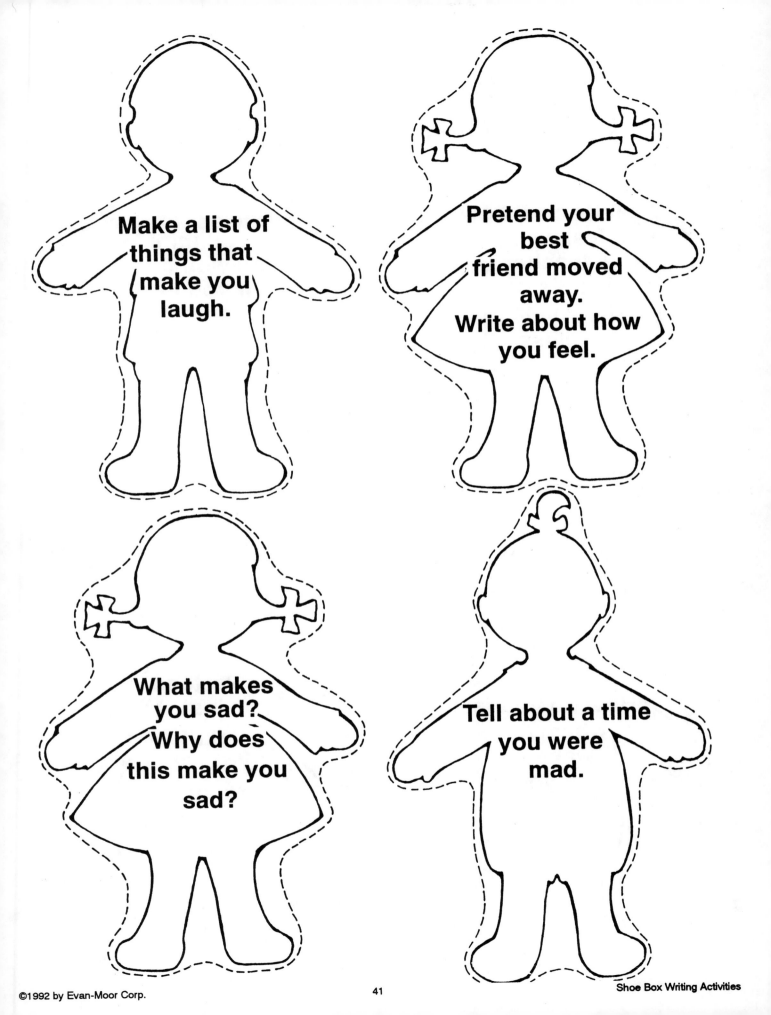

Make a list of things that make you laugh.

Pretend your best friend moved away. Write about how you feel.

What makes you sad? Why does this make you sad?

Tell about a time you were mad.

Shoe Box Writing Activities

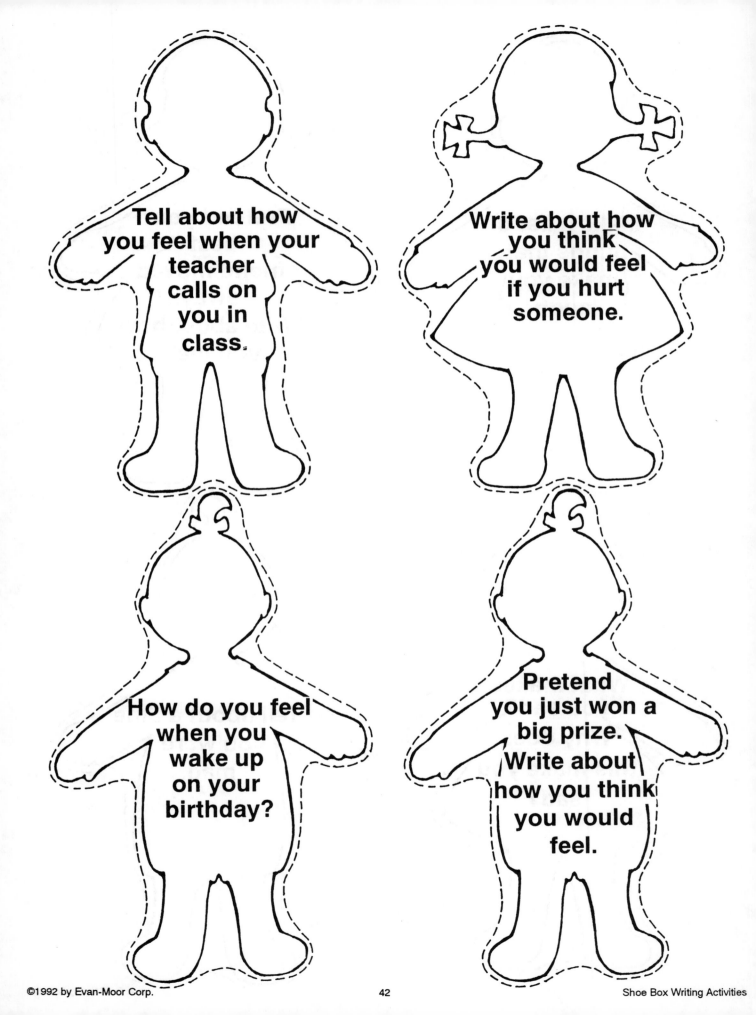

Tell about how you feel when your teacher calls on you in class.

Write about how you think you would feel if you hurt someone.

How do you feel when you wake up on your birthday?

Pretend you just won a big prize. Write about how you think you would feel.

Shoe Box Writing Activities

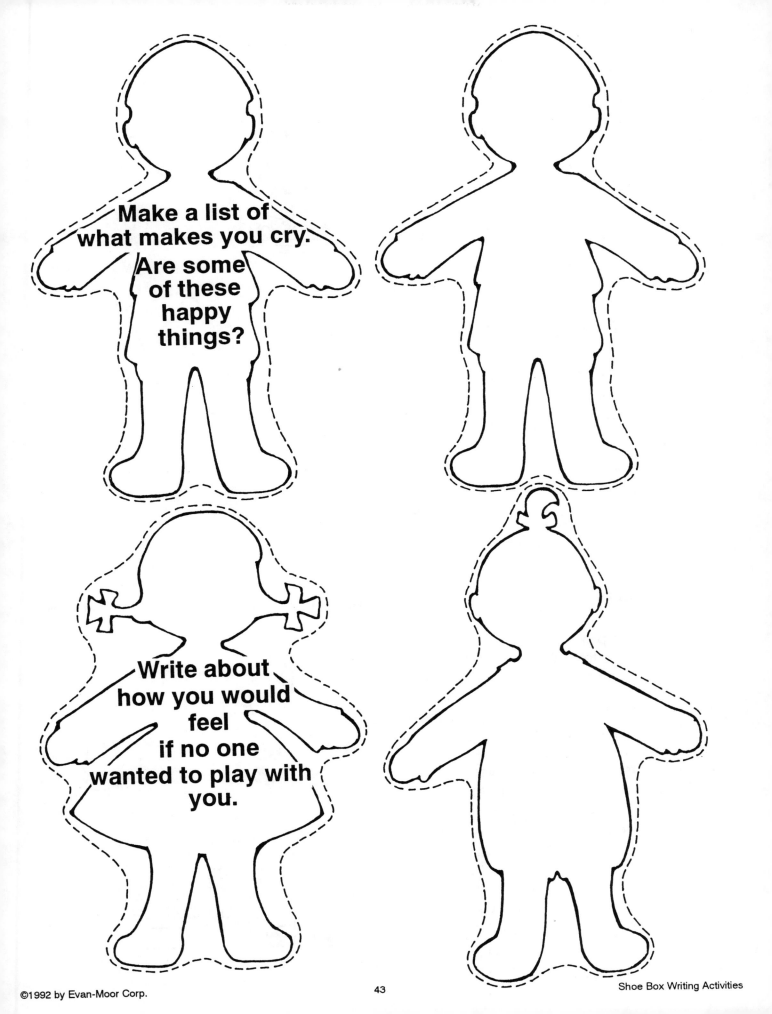

**Make a list of
what makes you cry.
Are some
of these
happy
things?**

**Write about
how you would
feel
if no one
wanted to play with
you.**

Shoe Box Writing Activities

Poetry

Use the frog box and the fly shapes to encourage children to write poems about the topics shown on the flies.

Preparing the Center:

1. Cover the shoe box and lid in Contact paper or butcher paper.

2. Use the frog pattern on page 45. Laminate the frog or cover it with clear Contact paper. Cut it out and attach it to the box with double-sided tape. Use an Exacto blade to cut out the hole in the frog's middle.

3. Reproduce the flies (pages 47-49) on card stock or copy paper. Laminate the pieces. Cut out the flies and place them in the frog shoe box.

4. Place the box in an easily accessible place. Provide a supply of pencils, crayons, writing paper, and drawing paper. You may want to add special pencils (bright colors, ones with frog or insect patterns, ones with frogs or insects on the end) for children to use at the writing center.

Have one or two children work at this center at a time.

Write Simple Poems:

1. Have the child pick a fly from the frog's mouth. He/She must read the card to find out the topic. There is also a rhyming word box on the fly.

2. He/She should make up rhyming sentences using words from the word box.

3. The child then chooses the sentences that make the best rhyme. The poem can be as short as two sentences.

kite
fly   buy
sky   by
high try

Kite
I went to buy
A Kite to fly
Way up in
the sky.

Frog
Pattern

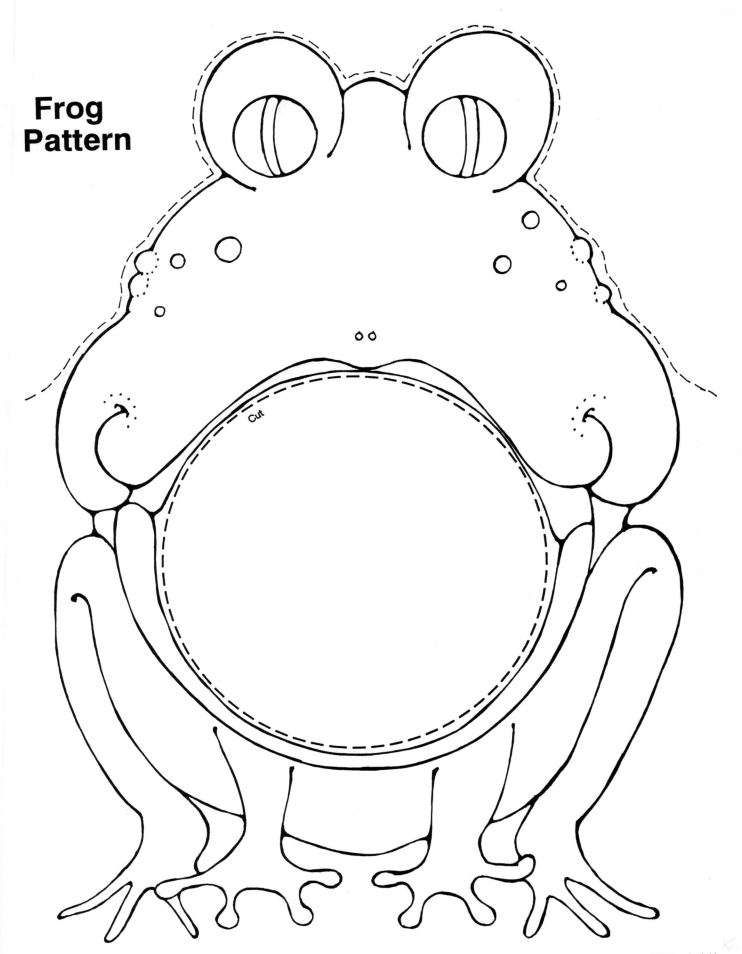

Cut

Shoe Box Writing Activities

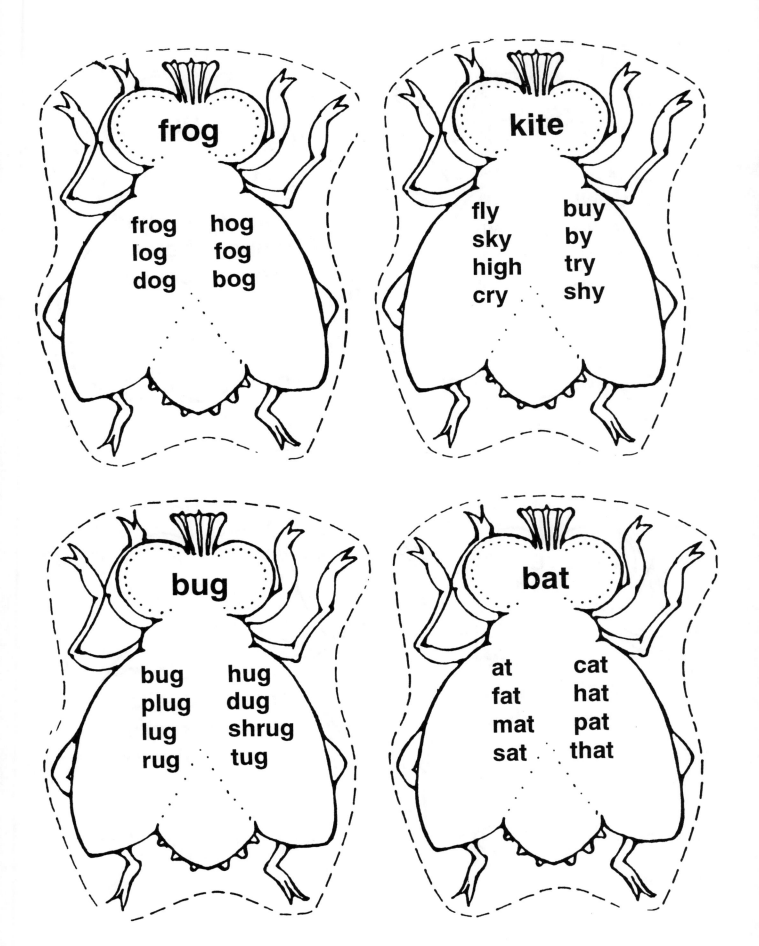

frog

frog	hog
log	fog
dog	bog

kite

fly	buy
sky	by
high	try
cry	shy

bug

bug	hug
plug	dug
lug	shrug
rug	tug

bat

at	cat
fat	hat
mat	pat
sat	that

Shoe Box Writing Activities

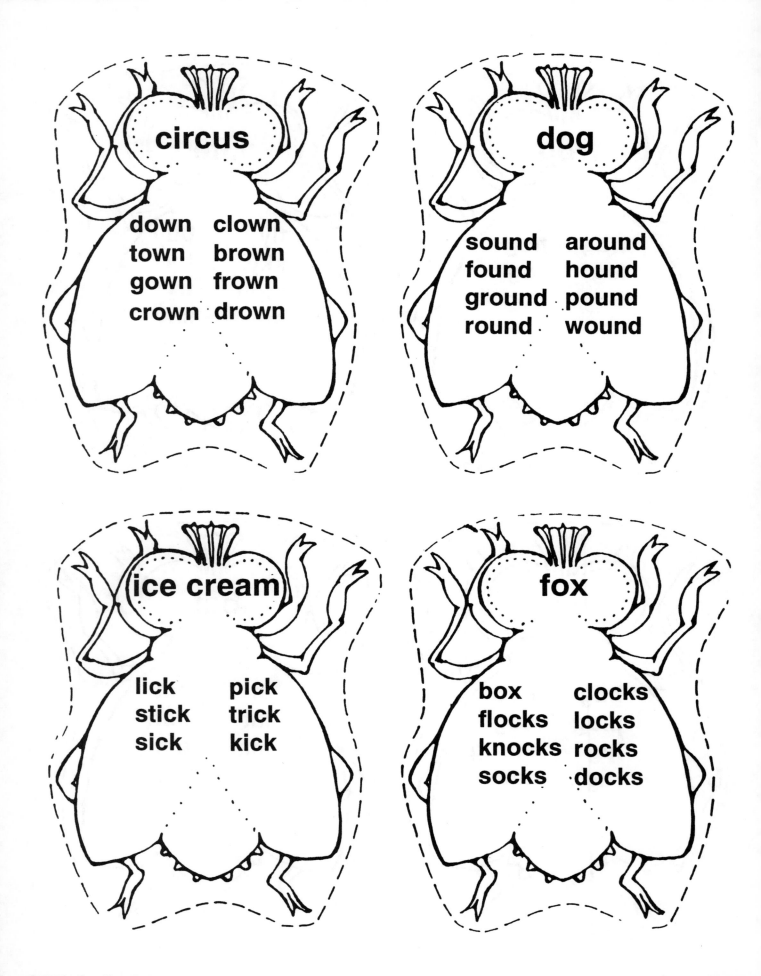

circus

down	clown
town	brown
gown	frown
crown	drown

dog

sound	around
found	hound
ground	pound
round	wound

ice cream

lick	pick
stick	trick
sick	kick

fox

box	clocks
flocks	locks
knocks	rocks
socks	docks

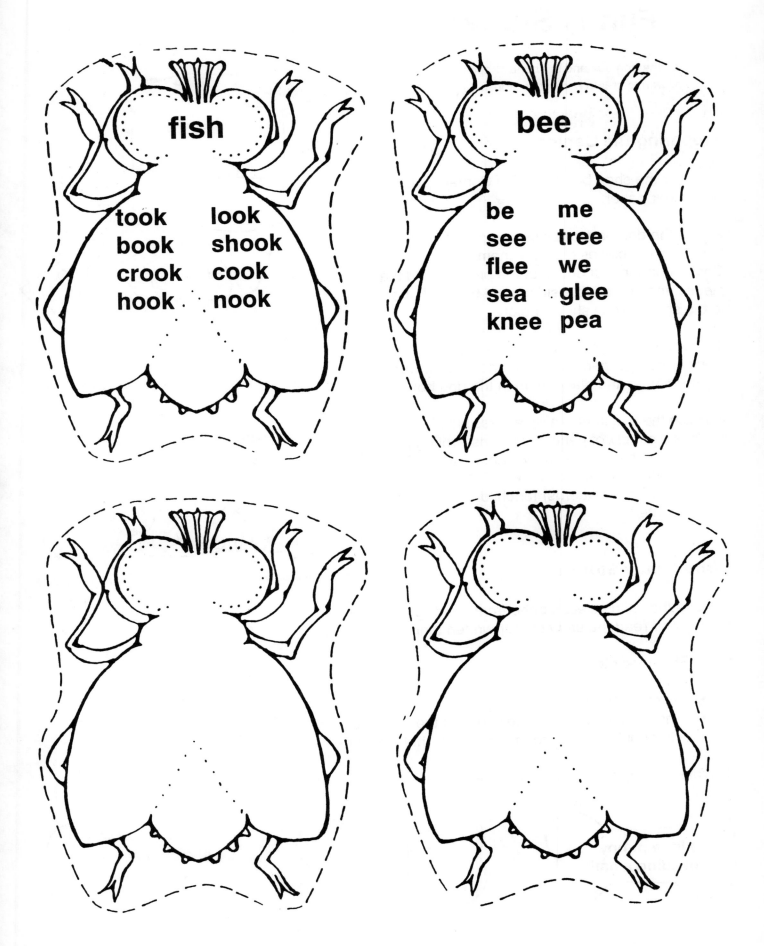

fish

took	look
book	shook
crook	cook
hook	nook

bee

be	me
see	tree
flee	we
sea	glee
knee	pea

49

Funny Stories

Use the dog box and the bone shapes to encourage children to create humorous stories.

Preparing the Center:

1. Cover the shoe box and lid in Contact paper or butcher paper.

2. Use the dog pattern pieces on pages 51 and 53. Laminate the pieces or cover them with clear Contact paper. Cut out all of the pieces. Fold the pieces and use double-sided tape to attach them to the shoe box as shown below.

3. Reproduce the bones (pages 55-57) on card stock or copy paper. Laminate the pieces. Cut out the bones and place them in the dog box.

4. Place the box in an easily accessible place. Provide a supply of pencils, crayons, writing paper, and drawing paper. You may want to add special pencils (bone shaped, ones with dog heads, ones with dog or bone patterns) for children to use at the writing center.

Have one or two children work at this center at a time.

Write Funny Stories:

1. Have the child select a bone from the dog's tummy and read the story starter written there.

2. He/She needs to think about...

- why the character is already funny
- what could happen in the situation that would be funny
- what could happen to the character that would be funny

3. Write a funny short story about the character. Illustrate the funniest part of the story.

a little puppy needing a bath

a clown in a circus

a sleepy boy trying to stay awake

Shoe Box Writing Activities

Dog Pattern - Head

Fold

Cut

Cut

Cut

Fold

Fold

Fold

Fold

Cut

Fold

Cut

Fold

Shoe Box Writing Activities

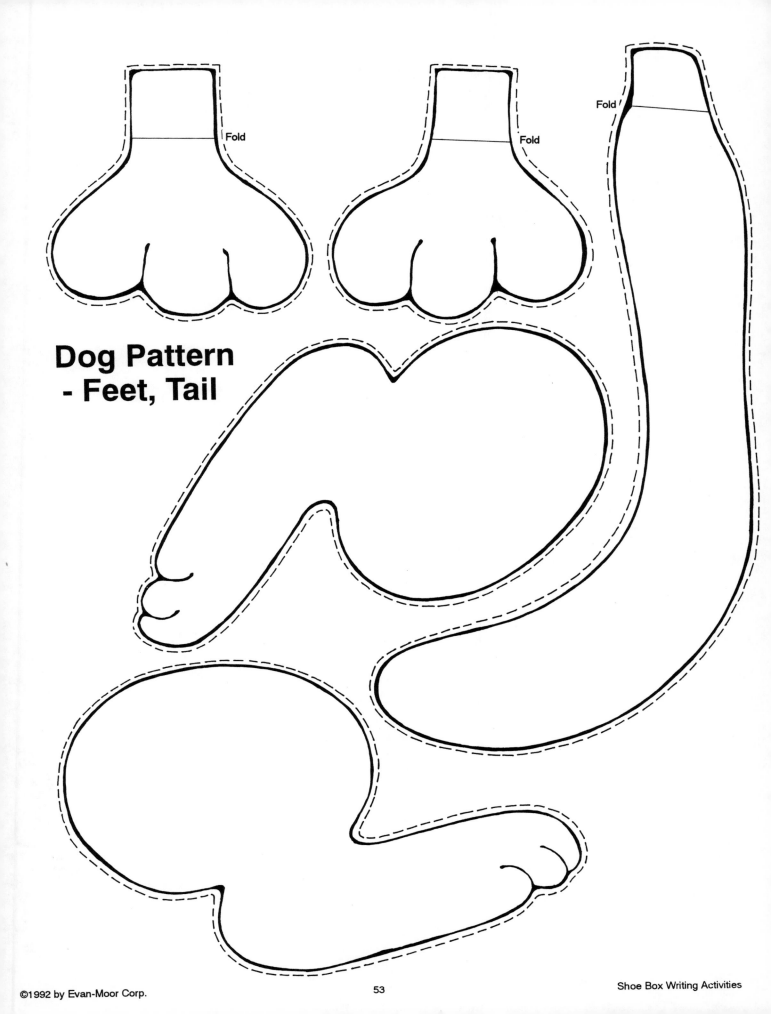

Dog Pattern
- Feet, Tail

Fold

Fold

Fold

Shoe Box Writing Activities

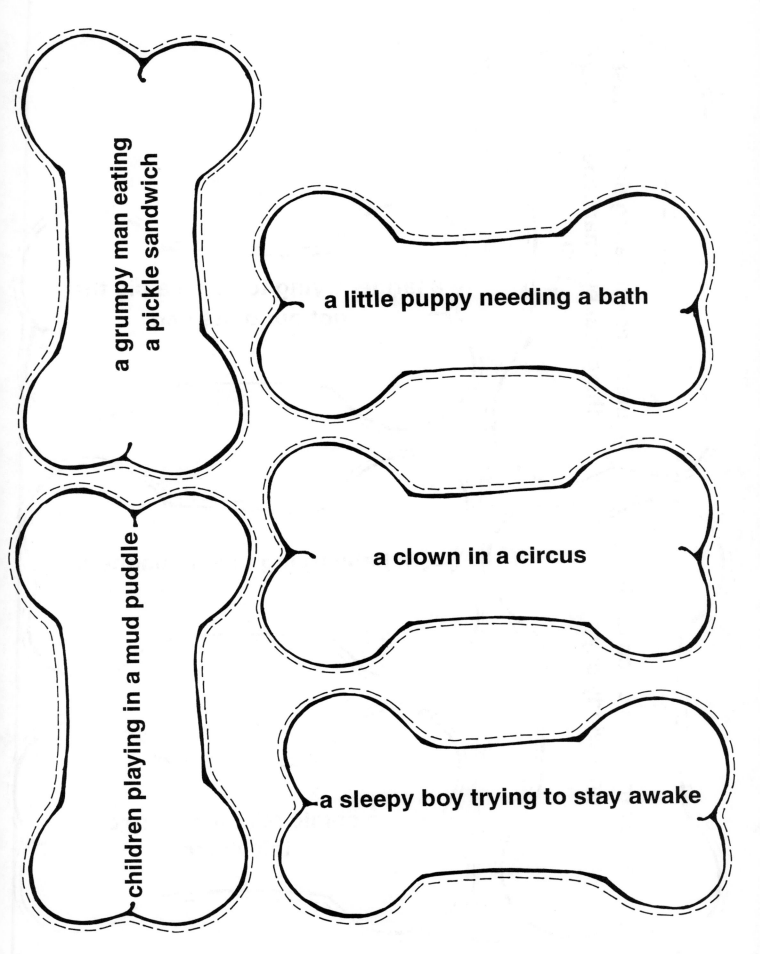

a grumpy man eating
a pickle sandwich

a little puppy needing a bath

children playing in a mud puddle

a clown in a circus

a sleepy boy trying to stay awake

Shoe Box Writing Activities

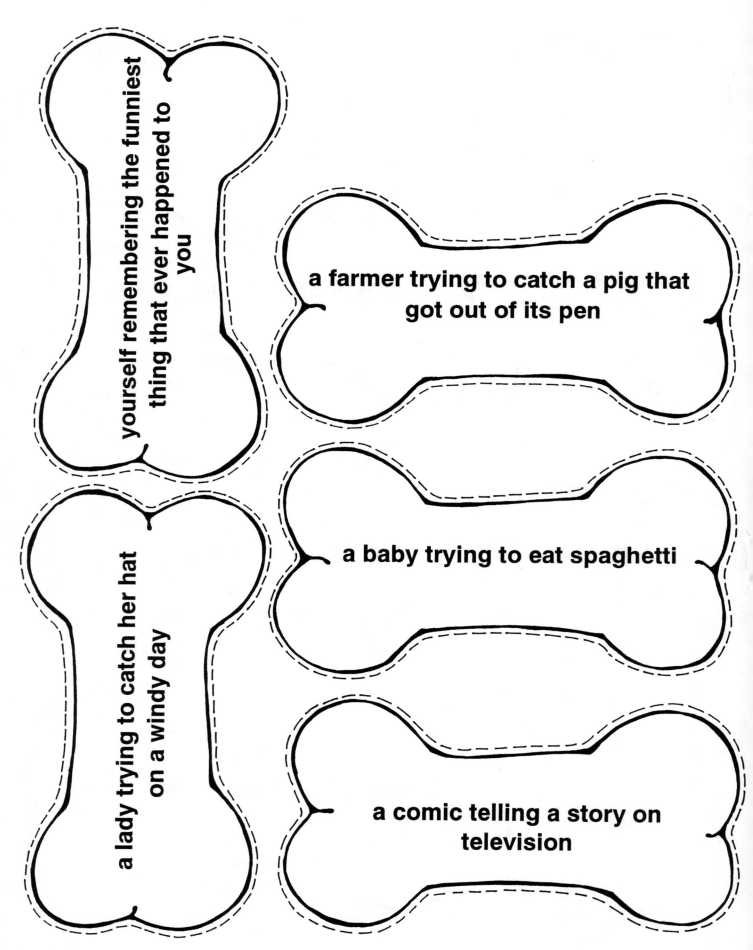

yourself remembering the funniest thing that ever happened to you

a farmer trying to catch a pig that got out of its pen

a lady trying to catch her hat on a windy day

a baby trying to eat spaghetti

a comic telling a story on television

Shoe Box Writing Activities

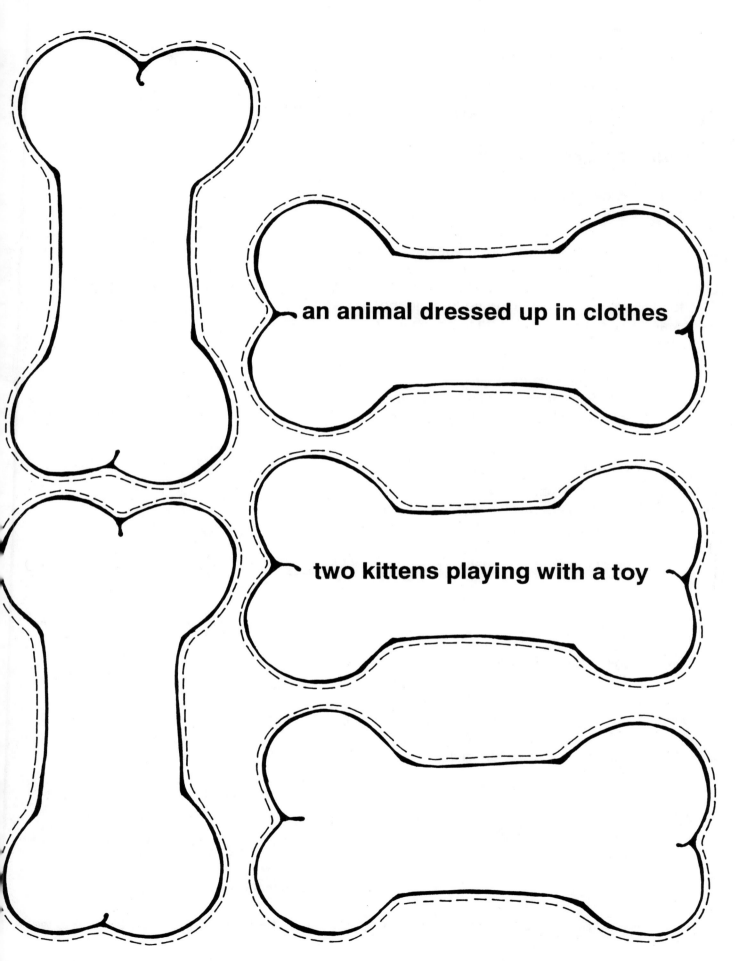

an animal dressed up in clothes

two kittens playing with a toy

Riddles

Use the chicken box and the egg and chick shapes to encourage children to create their own riddles. This is an excellent way to practice using descriptive language.

Preparing the Center:

1. Cover the shoe box and lid in Contact paper or butcher paper.

2. Use the chicken pattern pieces on pages 59 and 61. Laminate the pieces or cover them with clear Contact paper. Cut out all of the pieces. Use an Exacto blade to cut the slit in the head. Fold the pieces and use double-sided tape to attach them to the shoe box as shown below.

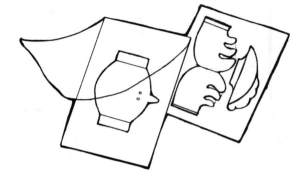

3. Reproduce the chicks and eggs (pages 63-65) on card stock or copy paper. Laminate the pieces. Cut out the eggs and chicks and place them in the chicken box.

4. Place the box in an easily accessible place. Provide a supply of pencils, crayons, writing paper, and drawing paper. You may want to add special pencils (bright colors, chicken and egg patterns, ones with chicken heads or eggs on the end) for children to use at the writing center.

Write Riddles:

Have one or two children work at this center at a time.

1. Have the child pick a chick and two eggs from the chicken box.

2. He/She must write a riddle about the subject on the chick including the information asked for on the eggs. (More information may be given, but they must include at least what is asked for on the eggs.)

What can it do?

Write a riddle about a chicken.

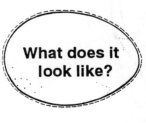
What does it look like?

3. He/She then draws the answer to the riddle on the back of the paper on which the riddle is written.

 Shoe Box Writing Activities

Pattern - Chicken Head

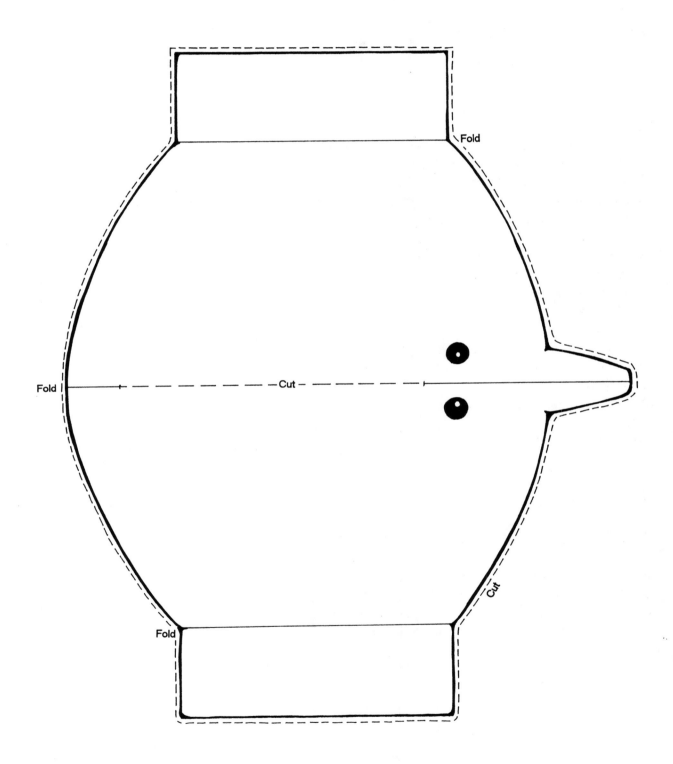

59

Chicken Pattern - Comb, Wings

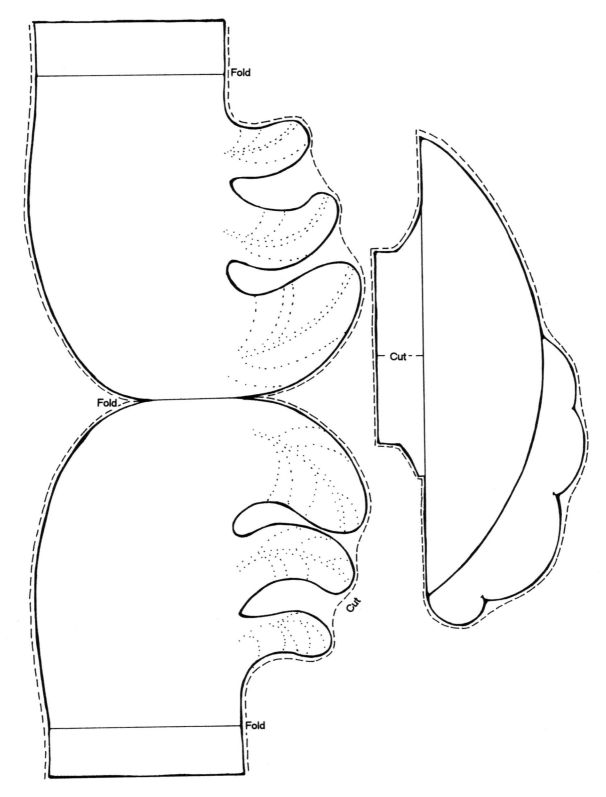

Fold

Fold

Cut

Cut

Fold

Shoe Box Writing Activities

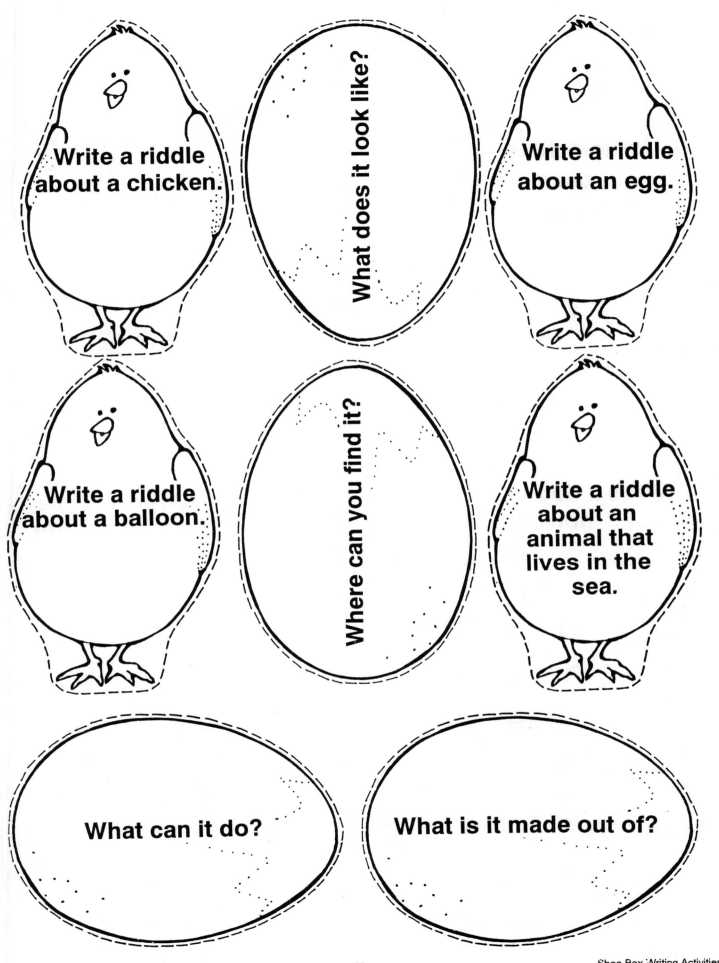

Write a riddle about a chicken.

What does it look like?

Write a riddle about an egg.

Write a riddle about a balloon.

Where can you find it?

Write a riddle about an animal that lives in the sea.

What can it do?

What is it made out of?

Shoe Box Writing Activities

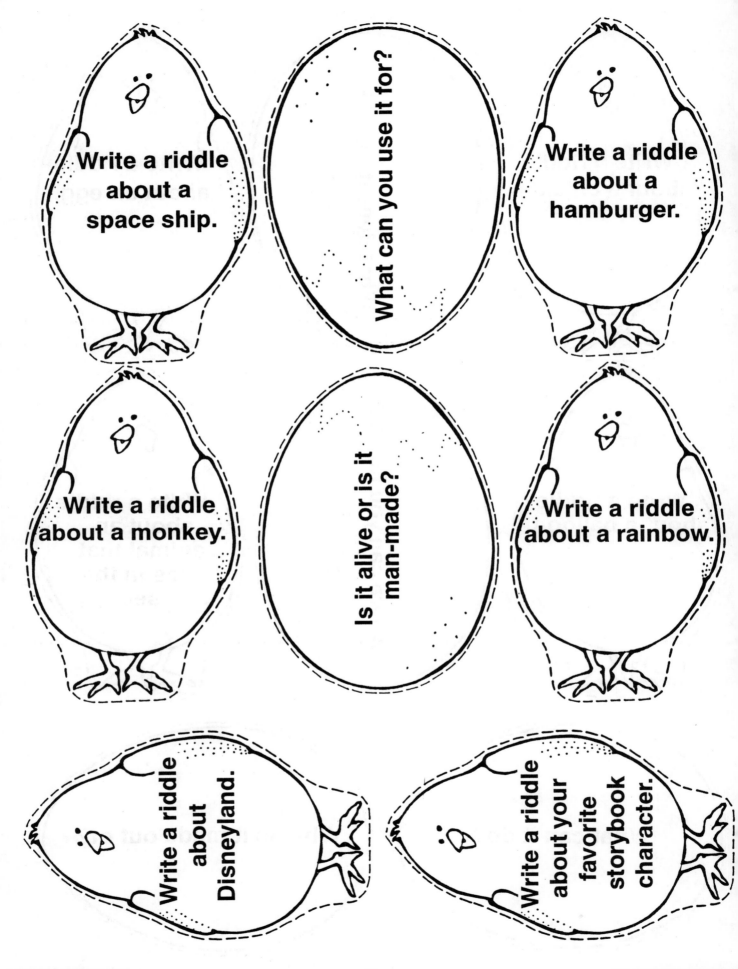

Write a riddle
about a
space ship.

What can you use it for?

Write a riddle
about a
hamburger.

Write a riddle
about a monkey.

Is it alive or is it
man-made?

Write a riddle
about a rainbow.

Write a riddle
about
Disneyland.

Write a riddle
about your
favorite storybook
character.

Shoe Box Writing Activities